Little Fires Hiding

Poems by

Jason Baldinger and James Benger

Kung Fu Treachery Press
Rancho Cucamunga, CA

Copyright (c) Jason Baldinger, James Benger, 2018
First Edition 1 3 5 7 9 10 8 6 4 2
ISBN: 978-1-946642-69-1
LCCN: 2018955397

Design, edits and layout: John T. Keehan, Jr.
Cover art: Jon Dowling
Author photos: Ethan Meyer, Hannah Benger
All rights reserved. No part of this publication may be reproduced or transmitted in any form or by any means, electronic or mechanical, including photocopying, recording or by info retrieval system, without prior written permission from the author.

Some of these poems have appeared in *Your One Phone Call, In Between Hangovers, Zombie Logic Review, Winedrunk Sidewalk,* and in the Low Ghost Anthology *Unconditional Surrender*

The poem *Josh Gibson Didn't Die For Your Sins* contains an excerpt from Bob Pajich's *Bloomfield Driver* from the book *The Trolleyman* (LowGhost Press)

CONTENTS

Winter 1979 / 1

We Worked Retail Through the Holidays / 4

The Hymn to Truck Nuts and Quantum Theory / 6

One Night / 8

Tuesday When the Lights Dim / 10

Aftertaste / 11

Wilmerding / 13

Jay / 14

Ghost Train Blues / 15

Boxcars / 17

Bluebirds at Rest Stops, Bluebirds for Waitresses / 19

11:38 p.m. At the Waffle House / 21

Ostriches and Camels / 23

Caged / 25

The Hymn to Boredom / 26

Drops / 28

Pittsburgh is a Real Place / 30

Machine / 32

At the Blue Haven / 34

Fraud / 36

Hymn to Garfield Hill / 38

Those Nights / 39

Zevjeli / 41

Correspondence / 43

Spahr Avenue / 45

Trowel / 46

A Remembrance of Andrew Carnegie on the
   125th Anniversary of the Battle of Homestead / 47

Pennies / 49

The Great Pittsburgh Pierogie Race N'at / 51

Batting Cleanup / 53

Josh Gibson Didn't Die For Your Sins / 57

Ballad / 58

Father's Day / 60

Just Visiting / 63

Cousins Bar / 65

At a Hole In the Wall Bar, December, 2002 / 67

The Night the Fireflies Taught Dave Brubeck
   to Keep Time / 70

This Is It / 72

Maybe a Mantra / 73

The Park / 75

You know the truth! The very water I baptized you with child was grey from the smoke of the mill! The truth is in your bones!

        -Father Dahr
           from Philip Bonosky's *Burning Valley*

Out of sorrow entire worlds have been built,
Out of longing great wonders have been willed

        -Nick Cave, *Are You the One*
         I've Been Waiting For

Winter 1979

corner of Beethoven and Apollo
hanging drywall in a warehouse
no running water
piss in a bucket
scan the east side of the city

shake dry wall dust out of my hair
the sun in this city
is the strange case of Jekyll and Hyde

when it's grey
with the brutal winter light
it could still be hell with the lid off

when it's sunshine
especially in the spring
especially in the fall
I swear it's the Garden of Eden

today, as I look
at the Immaculate Heart of Mary
it's both, sometimes at the same time

Pellegrino used to live down the street
late 70's, he's got his stories out
I can't keep dates straight

let's say winter '79
he climbed that Douglas Fir
on the hillside, drunk
cut twelve feet off the tree
so his wife could have
the Christmas she wanted

he tells me about Chessie
a Polish drunk a few hairs over five feet
who stuttered
and played the accordion
he fired howitzers during the great war
his brain never recovered

his sister was in an institution
after his parents died
he couldn't afford it
so he moved her in with him
lived off her social security checks

she died near the end of the month
he didn't call the cops
he didn't call the coroner
waited days till her next check came
bought a ton of beer
drank himself silly
then called the coroner
who couldn't tell when she died
her skin was wax, her ears were black

they covered her in a sheet
took her away
while Chessie rambled
he swore he fed her breakfast that morning

Chessie claimed he married Spanish Ann
who no one ever saw
but when he mentioned her
he'd wheeze in nasal voice
Blue Spanish eyes
tears falling from your Spanish eyes
it was nothing like Humperdinck

alcohol got the better of Chessie
he lost the house, taxes and loans
no more iron city pounders
he died alone
in one of those goddamn government rest homes

—Baldinger

We Worked Retail Through the Holidays

We would ride through the
ice and slush in my old beater,
tires bald, hard and uniquely
un-round enough to be a hazard
even in the best of conditions.

Skidding at the lights, always
having to keep a foot on the gas,
otherwise it'd die, and who knew
if I'd ever be able to get it to
turn over again, huge icicles
would drop from the poles above
and blast into a universe of shards
on the hood, glowing in the
reds and the moon.

Whenever we got to where we
were going, if we stayed too long,
the doors would freeze and the only
way in would be to pry the hatchback
open with a screwdriver and a
boozy three a.m. prayer.

We'd make it back to our beds in time
for two or three hours of fitful,
nauseous sleep before we returned
to exchange unwrapped holiday gifts
for cash and cards, smiling through
bloodshot eyes, rolling stomachs and
wistful memories of broken mattresses.

We lived only one shade north of
poverty and we worried about everything,
but damn, did we have a good time.

—Benger

The Hymn to Truck Nuts and Quantum Theory

drinking with Renee and Nikki
at the Park House, we're talking
truck nuts, wondering why
they don't come with a dick attached
they could come uncircumcised
your truck could have a bris every day
as you barrel along the American highway

the ladies ask why there isn't truck clits
or truck assholes for that fact
why can't we have cars
that are anatomically correct
there are napkin drawings
schematics, I'm not sure which
future millionaire got to take home

I start to tell Renee a story, now a poem
she's heard it before, this is the danger
when you write your life
instead it launches us into alternate timelines
the quantum fracturing that each of our
decisions leave, the endless possibilities
honeycombed across our universe

she says I should write a book
of alternate histories of myself
I can't fathom that obsessive endeavor
and I say so. Time is its own Pandora's Box
regret, the want to change the past
is a ridiculous human feeling
it's our choices, for whatever reason
that make us or leave us stranded

I thought about that history, that
quantum alternative, remembering being
twenty-three with a job offer, Acorn
I believe as a community organizer
twenty k a year, and a move
to Philadelphia for training

I was with a girl, getting started
on a relationship that would last
six years and change, my grandmother
was dying, it seemed like leaving
was the wrong thing to do that day

I called the guy back, a little tearful
not as free as I believed
truth or fiction
I went back to working in a bank
thirty-seven hours a week

—Baldinger

One Night

We sat,
stood,
ate,
swayed,
drank,
swayed some more,
sweated
and rocked
hours in the club.

Somewhat damp
overstayed welcome,
not spinning,
but not straight,
I erringly pilot us
down a one-lane
one-way crest of
the Northland
that ends in
nothing but trees
and no.

Unsteady reverse swerves,
we make it back
over the tracks.

Rainy railroaded missteps,
I dropped him at his place.

He shakes my hand,
hugs me like goodbye.
I say he can't lose me
that easy.

Watching him fade
into rearview rain,
I wonder if I lied.

—Benger

Tuesday When the Lights Dim

Buttercup walked in
after fighting with his wife
who keeps calling him lazy
he smokes at the end of the bar

Sean is on the floor
measuring black pipe
to hold up the counter
we just installed
he says his wife is an angel

Timmy is writing a liquor order
coughing hard
he's been nursing a coke
he says it's hard to wake up
every day with a hangover
for over thirty years

I'm heading to Home Depot
to get pipes cut and threaded
leaning on the bar
I'm waiting hard
outside the sun will be blinding

—Baldinger

Aftertaste

What's left of the
green plastic
army man who
drove a truck
in Germany is
slouched over the bar.

In the dim lighting,
it's hard to tell if
he's awake,
asleep, or
more than asleep.

A fourth or fifth
glass of bourbon,
neat sits in front of him,
the rim dangerously
close to his slowly
sinking forehead,
threatening to impale him
like all those near-miss
Nazi bullets.

He drinks alone every night,
surrounded by intoxicants
and the intoxicated,

all packaged and sold
long after his first
physical war ended.

He stirs, looks distastefully,
distrustfully at the glass, then
repeats the narrow-eyed
grimace when he catches a
glimpse of himself in the
mirror behind the bar.

Nothing tastes the same
as it used to.
Nothing but bourbon
and grudges.

—Benger

Wilmerding

sparrow's nests
hang on each letter
Valley Auto Parts

—Baldinger

Jay

A jay on his branch,
the wind in his feathers.
The branch swaying – just a little.
Some ice on the wood
and snow on the ground.

A maple leaf blows up,
dances in front of the bird's face.
Then the howling breeze
takes the leaf elsewhere.
Maybe to visit another jay.
The bird's eyes follow
the path of the leaf until it is
out of sight.

The bird contemplates the
higher branches of its tree
and the gray sky above.
The bird takes flight.
A journey known only to itself.

—Benger

Ghost Train Blues

chase mourning doves off rumble strips
cross the Little Miami
the taste of rain in Warren County

wetland jungles
count mayapples
count wild strawberries
blessed mosquitoes

Adena burial mounds
2600 years sacred sleep
buffalo soldiers
waterfalls

a stop sign on
a cattle guard
a refuse pile

road sign
Jesus is the son of God
who the fuck
are you trying
to convince?

a woman seated
stretched across

two plastic chairs
the parking lot
of the Cordele Motel

a proud heritage
in agriculture

four kids
ride two paint ponies
one with a broken wrist

strip mall Mexican restaurant

Taco Bell sign
lords over a
knee high wheat field
carnival rides
sleep in storage

shell of
a '40 Plymouth
stretched
on a trailer bed

hammer down
leap frog cars
from the passing lane
flicker of telephone poles
race the ghost train

—Baldinger

Boxcars

There are some boxcars that have
been sitting in the yard for decades.
You can always spot them amongst
the backdrop of the newer ones,
even the newer, but still
decommissioned ones.

The ones we're concerned with have
weeds growing up around them,
growing up on them,
growing up through them.
They're the ones that, no matter their
original color, they always end up
that rusty brown-red uncolor.
They have wooden floors that have
been gnawed by mice and rats and
termites and all other things.
Opossums have bred families in them.
Maybe there was a coyote that once
tried to get in because he could smell
small, warm flesh inside.

Back when the boxcar was young,
back before the rust and the rodents,
back before the weeds and the
long, monotonous nothingness,

it would glide down the track,
oiled and glorious in its precision.
The boxcar would haul all manner of things,
not the least of which was the occasional
man trying to escape.
Escape the law,
escape the bottle,
the family,
maybe he only needed to escape himself.
Regardless of when the man would
finally hop off and back into the world,
the boxcar would keep gliding on,
doing its job,
serving its purpose.
Until the day it didn't.

Now the days in the yard have
long outnumbered the ones on the rails.
Birds have called it their family home
for generations upon generations.
To them, the boxcar has always been there.
A Grand Canyon.
A Stonehenge.
But it hasn't.

There are some boxcars that have
been sitting in the yard for decades,
but once they rode.

—Benger

Bluebirds at Rest Stops, Bluebirds for Waitresses

in a rest stop inside the Illinois border
walking out of the bathroom
the attendant says
is that Woody Allen on your shirt?
it's Charles Bukowski I say
she says *who's that*
then asks me to trade her shirts
in the Calivan
Collins cracks us up
doing his best Allen impersonation
reading from *Women*

this morning in a diner
technically, by the sign, a shoppe
the waitress asks
who's that on your shirt?
it's Charles Bukowski I say
she says *who's that*
he's a poet
is he your favorite poet?
no, one of them
she writes his name on her order pad
she has a pretty but vacant smile
she says she'll check him out
how does it feel to educate people? she asks

good, I said, trying to figure out
how to talk about bluebirds
far more interested in
a three egg omelet
stuffed with rare roast beef
smothered in horseradish

—Baldinger

11:38 p.m. At the Waffle House

The coffee tastes of burnt rubber,
but at least it's hot. Walking the
narrow aisles (some of the portlier
patrons rub elbows from adjacent
booths) she runs the pot to the
man in the corner. He scrawls on
his yellow legal pad, number two
pencil calling out noises fit for a
late 1990's underground rave. She
hates how the harsh fluorescents
unflinchingly highlight the increasing
grey streaks in her frizzy hair.
Without asking, she refills his non-
descript, standard-issue mug to the
brim. The outside of that brim sports
a brown stain in the shape of the man's
bottom lip. She stands beside the table
for a moment, expecting some sign of
gratitude. He never lifts his head from
his work. The pencil never stops
etching lines into paper. His head is
always cocked at just the right angle so
she can never quite see what he's writing.
She notices that the pencil and the paper
are almost the same shade of yellow, and

that is somehow more obnoxious than the
hellish lights, and all of the undesirable
diner guests beneath them. She walks
away. He will tip her. Always does.
And it will be a good one. She knows.
He does this every night.

—Benger

Ostriches and Camels

White Bliss scratched
Mr Munson scratched
Spicebomb change overcheck
The American Kings are on at ten
complete with lights and Morricone's theme
The Good, The Bad, and The Ugly

Elvis hips swing, the velocity of slicked back hair
ancient couples in matching t-shirts,
matching socks, shiny shoes
swing, get low on carpets
that are an ocean on the right drugs

Jimmy Reed covers as the Penguins start
period three, on one TV a Latino jockey
rides with an American flag
they superimpose him and the flag
layers of patriotism, all the glory

Rickenbacker and Gretch
pretty in the backlight
nurses and business men
leopard prints and sequins
do the shimmy, the swim
the bunny hop, white hair bobs
along to *Louie Louie*

The Penguins are going down
TV advertises stud fees
ostriches and camels June sixteenth
Corona bottles turn red, lost in lights
as patrons cheer the first set
shiny shoes still shiny

A man from Buffalo says
Why are we even looking at ice
it's goddamn fucking June?

—Baldinger

Caged

I keep getting split-second
glimpses of him,
stained shirt and sad eyes.
The door swings on its
weighted but unbalanced hinges
and at its most open,
I see him.
He soundlessly prepares the
greasy bar food for the
drunks and drinkers,
a flit of a small radio
momentary overtaking the jukebox.
I watch for each swing
of the door,
hoping to catch some new
element of his existence.
Over a carelessly carried
plate of fried pickles,
I catch his eyes.
His pupils emote a
wordless desperation.
Then the door swings shut.

—Benger

The Hymn to Boredom

we passed the factory with roof collapsed
    passed the house she grew up in
        then another house she grew up

she didn't want to go down that road
heroin is out of control there
anyone there is hustling
        is turning tricks
        is looking to score

she lost the wheel to her car here
her virginity there, these are small town
stories, I deal in stories
she asks again if I'm bored
not the first time over
the past few days she has
I'm not, the world is timelines
        the world is stories

I was riding around with another friend
a few months back catching up
talking Jesus and serial killers
she worried I may be bored

this world moves too fast
we chase tails in circles
    around uncertain futures
I love listening, I love to be still
it's rare I find myself bored
when I do, it's welcome
a respite, a moment I can
shut off my crazy brain
enjoy living in just one moment

—Baldinger

Drops

This trip keeps taking us
down weird roads.
Or maybe it's Rex's
unfounded hatred of GPS
that keeps bringing us
to these places.

Not that computers are infallible,
but we, in all our map-reading ability,
surely ain't neither.

Pavement cracked almost to gravel,
traffic signs graffitied to the point
you now know why they made you take
that shape recognition test
to get your DL,
balls-out daylight,
yet guys with open forties and
barely-concealed glocks
lounge on the curb.

A girl no older than five
pedals her trike from the
front of the dilapidated church,
makes it to the middle of the street.

Then her ride drops the front wheel;
the wheel rolls to the gutter,
the girl and the trike stay put.

Show in the windshield,
I slow to a crawl.

The girl gets off the
obviously scavenged banana seat,
proceeds to kick the incomplete trike
with the vitriol of a much older person.

I can't help but laugh and think,
You and me both, kid,
you and me both.

—*Benger*

Pittsburgh is a Real Place

the kids on the stoop ogle
a Lamborghini, shout at passersby
is this yours?
mockingbirds across the street
from some recent upscale place
I remember when it was a coffee shop
when BYOB shows rolled deep in the night
back when this neighborhood was *dangerous*

I sit down, suburban version of the original
stuck out, sore thumb in the city
the bartender flirts with a guy at the end
two guys talk places, all the places
they talk companies and big paydays
they aren't from around here
one says *I don't know, Pittsburgh is a real place*

the two guys on the other side of me
talk about how Garfield has changed
they talk about some accident that happened
outside years ago, they tally up and coming
neighborhoods, like me, they don't make
enough to buy in, they believe they can

on the way home air is heavy
or I am heavy, the sunset is dusted
muted. I don't want to buy into any
dream sold American anymore. It was never
meant for me anyway, I've made
my own dream in the cracks
I don't care that America forgot me

—Baldinger

Machine

In this place of plastic,
its shiny unreality,
unblemished promise of
everything we can't have
would we even want it?
we sip overpriced beer,
sold a couple degrees
below freezing,
'cause colder is better,
if you don't want to
taste it.

Snow falls outside,
white flakes of indifference
we can catch through the window
between the strobes.

After too many drinks
we'll leave,
find the pavement,
the tires,
the seats
frozen,
slow blooded,
indifferent.

Machines don't care;
they freeze your beer,
get you from here to there,
incinerate you when you're done,
so you can sit on a mantle,
or be scattered somewhere.

Machines do it all
with cold, scalpel precision,
and we meatbags stand
dumb and bovine in the way.

The waitress in the shirt
meant for a preteen
asks if we want another,
manicured nails on shoulders.

Everything's plastic,
everything's automated,
preplanned,
calculated,
and our fallible flesh
falls in every time.
And the machine
gets us
again.

—Benger

At the Blue Haven

sky opens
familiar summer squall
The Blue Haven
electric neon smothers outside eaves
hisses and hums in the rain
the soundtrack to backseat cocaine

smog veil opens
on a five dollar cover
outside sign said
Glitz this Saturday

evidently the Quite Riot
cover is Glitz
bartender tells me they used to be 9-1-1

the bikers have no idea
why we're over dressed
Ian paid the cover for the bride
and groom yet to arrive

seated, exhausted
how many drinks have I had
since the industrial hell mouth
gave birth to ceremony?

I can't remember
I don't care
I drink myself
disappointed
sober

fingers looped in suspenders
bride and groom arrive
take shots
I nurse workers tears
Sweet Child of Mine
half step down
limps without a second guitar

someone is high school catching up
someone asks for a tampon
someone asks about the wedding
we pick the bones of a commemorative box of cookies
debate to even odds the next song
it's a struggle as it breaks the verse
shit, I hadn't heard Trixter since 1990

tonight, our time machine falls off the table

—Baldinger

Fraud

When you're invited,
and you like the ones
doing the inviting,
and you've got no excuse,
nowhere else to be,
even if you know you don't belong,
you show.

Brown barn in nowhere,
dying haybales,
listless donkey in pen,
a rooster what thinks
he owns it all.

They had a lot of beer,
so much beer,
bar's always open
when the bar's a
stack of unattended coolers
on the porch.

Buzz running high,
they say their vows
in a field,
and it's right for them,
sun going down over the pines,

I feel good for them,
squeeze my wife's hand,
glad our friends have found
what we have.

Reception is cowboy hats and boots;
hillbilly jam circle.
Groom offers me a spare guitar,
I politely decline,
fearing being found out
as a musical fraud.

I had band practice yesterday,
we've been jamming and gigging together
since before the turn of the century;
pretty comfortable with a neck in my grip,
but put me around strangers
who know what they're doing,
I'm still a novice,
wishing I knew.

—Benger

Hymn to Garfield Hill

six am
there's pizza in the fridge
why don't we grab a slice

my roommate left for work
there's no reason to grab at garment scatter
it's too hot for clothes anyway

leaning against the counter
the rise above water tower
wears the first seconds of July sun

cool air from the fridge, cold pizza on the stove
two arms wrapped around one body
face buried in her hair, she laughs
chews mouth open, breaks
then passes pieces over her shoulder

why don't we get back in bed
shake the birds out of
the trees one more time

let's let hymns bloom
in the sky over Garfield Hill
before sweat stings our eyes to sleep

—*Baldinger*

Those Nights

I romanticize those nights
of booze and drugs
and late night art.

Playing gigs in Lawrence,
afterpartying hard,
coming back to the
apartment in Kansas City,
buzzed, but ready for the move,
hitting the bar,
shooting pool,
throwing darts,
talking shit,
we'd end up at the
apartment complex playground,
a case of Red Stripe,
riding the swings,
speaking to the
youthful midsummer
glory of it all.

I romanticize those nights,
but tend to omit the part
where my buddy was
passed out and drooling

in front of the Toxic Avenger
at 4 a.m.,
while I puked into a plastic grocery sack
because I couldn't afford
a fucking trash can.

I'd wake to be at the gas station
at 6 a.m. for my shift.
How did I do it?

Sometimes I romanticize those nights,
but those days are long gone,
and best left for the kids
who have yet to find
what I have.

—Benger

Zevjeli

they're scattered
hunkie bars lost to time
dispersed on goat path hills
dotted across valleys, buried in hollers
they are heaven when found

mirrored walls, fake flowers
no dust, no soot, so still
nothing changed since 1974

the owner talks across the bar
the elderly couples here for tonight's
spaghetti specials, one guy asks
about meatballs, they won't win any contest

I've heard the spiel before
Steve at the Bloomfield Bridge Tavern
does it best, when he wants to give you
a free shot of blackberry brandy
Sheila or Red Bob or Mark called
this is an ice cream topping
we don't sell ice cream anymore though
sip this don't shoot it
Nostrovia my friend

she says she doesn't drink
like her father, still there
are several shots, I can pick one
Slivovitz, plum brandy firewater
she says are you sure
the couple at the bar ask if I'm sure
I nod, she pours, Zevjili
it punches my tongue
not a shooter, eyes burn
back to front, little fires hiding

she says how is it? I blink,
sip my beer, sip again
take another nip, say Slivovitz
this is like Ouzo or Tequila
it's the drink that
crawls under skin
leads to a place of forgetting

unsteady towards the door, bluffing
the old man says make sure you drive
across the river, watch out for the current
I got this, I'll drive under the river instead
his return face swims oddly
I shout again, Zevjili

—Baldinger

Correspondence

She's got a white lace
handkerchief that she's repeatedly
pulling out and dabbing at
her glistening forehead;
the booze sweats have
already set in.

She'd be pretty if it weren't
for all the tears running the
once heavy makeup
down into the glory land.

She started with fluorescent,
presumably fruity drinks, but
she's long since switched to
double shots of tequila,
no salt, no lime,
chased with a Diet Coke that
hasn't touched her painted lips
in three shots.

She's crying,
and drinking,
and sweating,
and writing
a long, long something.

It started with deliberate,
dainty curls, each one
punctuated by motionless thought,
but now the words come
fast and hard and violent.
She grips the pen
like an icepick.

She wipes her head again,
yellow, stinking sweat,
motions to the
man behind the bar
for another round,
then goes back to
etching hate into paper.

Before the next drink comes,
between violent letters,
she mutters:
Fucker,
or maybe it was:
Father.

—Benger

Spahr Avenue

sparrows turn
to fireworks
every time I crack
the back door

squirrels
only mind
when I power on
the wet saw

hands vibrate
through ceramic tile
inches from the blade

I wonder how
many syllables
are in each of my fingers

—*Baldinger*

Trowel

Smoothing the wet concrete,
my father tells me
the trowel I'm using
belonged to my great-grandfather.

I grip the handle and wonder
if some of the man's sweat
is still hidden away in the
wooden pores.

In the simple act
of using a tool,
I'm instantly connected
in a wholly new way
to a man I never met,
a man of who's name I'm not even sure,
but a man upon who's existence,
mine is predicated.
All I really know is that he was
my mother's father's father.

I wipe the blade clean
and look at flat patch of wet concrete
and wonder if he would look at my job
and be proud.

—Benger

A Remembrance of Andrew Carnegie on the 125th Anniversary of the Battle of Homestead

Sunday drives, Hudson Valley
south on Nine past Ossining
its old suburban money gone

I never pass up a cemetery
especially in Washington Irving land
with tree spirits alive and well
where an iron Headless Horseman
still as sculpture lurks among graves

I grab a map, historical burials
are a hobby of mine
I notice Samuel Gompers
founder of the American Federation of Labor
I notice Andrew Carnegie
that fucker died in Scotland
I'm sure

I find Gompers easily enough
Carnegie is next door
down an idyllic tree lined path
isolated from the peons
not as rich as this motherfucker
already gritting my teeth
I wonder what a post mortem
conversation between Gompers

and Carnegie would be
the pedestal, the plaque
before a large cross, lists
of philanthropic endeavors
echo hollow with a man
who came from a city of workers
that were firmly under his boot

I notice a smaller stone
covered in coins from aspiring
capitalists hoping to get lucky
what was it Steinbeck said
about embarrassed millionaires?

I make a call to a friend
hope for a suggestion
disobedience or vandalism
voicemail finds spitting fury
I settle, it would be easy
to piss on the grave
as I've done to George Bush's father
or Gilded Age financier Mark Hanna
it doesn't seem enough

I stew, fish quarter out
of pocket, rather than flip
I fling, I know I have no
super powers that can demolish
stone. I growl
Fuck you from the people of Homestead!

—Baldinger

Pennies

Some of us,
most of us
had listened to the records
beyond all repetition.

Not originally from
Kansas City,
I knew the name,
knew the music,
but perhaps didn't understand
the importance.

We all cram into a tiny car,
Angel, an out-of-towner
behind the wheel.
We excitedly,
reluctantly depart
39th and Bell,
head north.

None of us have been there,
something for which
we're all silently ashamed.
Signals cut out,
GPS convulses,

Angel suggests that Siri
needs to stop smoking the crack.

We make it there,
peaceful, windy green
in the mid-morning
spring sun.

And there he is,
six feet below,
just as he's always been,
seemingly waiting for us.

We pay our poetic respects
as a funeral procession
inches by down the one lane road,
too busy in their own grief
to see a circle of misfits with notebooks
speaking in turn
to a dead man.

The tree cover parts just over the grave,
and someone left a handful of pennies
as if they had fallen from heaven.

—Benger

The Great Pittsburgh Pierogie Race N'at

it was a playoff game at the Bloomfield Bridge Tavern
      the best place for a playoff game
it was Pirates and Cardinals
an empty bar, except for a group of friends
I don't remember which game it was
honestly, now I don't remember if they won
but I'm pretty sure it was Paulie's idea

they're home we should have our own
      pierogie race n'at
no one thought Sheila would take it seriously
      until the pierogies showed up
butter and onion dreams
Polish potato perfection

someone thought we should personalize
our pierogies. sharpies on toothpick polish flags
each pierogie an individual now
just like at the home games

when they cut to commercial
home half of the sixth
we each took a shot putt
of pierogie, it was less a race
more an Olympic event

the hallowed faithful
after twenty years of losing
send their playoff dreams down
the bar covered in butter

whichever pierogie made it
farthest won, I remember
that winning pierogie
a snail trail of animal fat
glistening under dim lights
lying still alone on the bar

sometimes losers get lucky
sometimes there's just a little hope
  that makes it worthwhile to sit
       to watch
       to cheer

       —Baldinger

Batting Cleanup

And then there was that time
when we got all new
computer and register systems
for the gas station.

The techs who installed the stuff
piled all the old crap in the back hallway,
behind the bathrooms,
blocking the way to the coolers
and the office.

Manager told me,
the sole employee on the
upcoming nightshift,
to get rid of the junk.

I'm sure he expected me
just chuck it in the dumpster
sometime between two and four a.m.;
that time when there's never any customers,
save the occasional tweaker or drunk,
that time when I was supposed to
deep-clean the cappuccino machines
and Windex down all the pumps,
but instead, usually found myself
eating free doughnuts,

flipping through magazines
and blasting whichever
punk or metal album was doing it for me that day.

Never one to miss an opportunity,
I called up a handful of friends,
a couple were former coworkers at the station.

There was a ladder leading to a
trap door to the roof.
We hauled ourselves,
the electronics,
some snacks from the shelves,
a case of 3.2 beer from the cooler
onto the gravelly lookout.

The stars were full bright,
casting alien glow
on the cornfield across the street.

The game was to get a decent buzz going,
pick your equipment
(remember to consider weight),
and see if you could sail it
all the way to the dumpster on the
other side of the parking lot.

No one made it.

Brilliant flashes of
motherboards,
screws,
tubes,
glass screens
shattering on the cracked pavement.

Our will to continue
outlasted the ammunition.

We took the party back down the ladder,
grabbed the push brooms from the hallway
and some aluminum from the shelves,
and played semi-drunk soup can shuffleboard
until the first customer of the morning rush
showed for her regular cup of sub-par mud.

While I rang her up, she informed me
that after seeing what we were doing,
she'd never buy food there again.

As the flow of patrons
went from old man pee
to Niagara Falls,
my compatriots headed off
for their jobs or beds.

The morning crew showed
during the first lull of the a.m..

Heading out the door,
hoping my twenty-two-year-old station wagon would start,
I informed the new kid that someone had
made a hell of a mess out by the dumpster;
he'd better get a broom.

—Benger

Josh Gibson Didn't Die for Your Sins
(for Bob Pajich)

Speedy's has angus burgers
two for five bucks
American Girl ends
crossing the Homestead Grays Bridge
spark a joint
Lunatic Fringe starts

the Little Bill
the Monongahela
on fire

a cloud farm
a cobalt sky

Pajich's stanza:
Pittsburgh is a unique place
it's the only city in the world
where you could cross three rivers
and still be lonely

Josh Gibson
didn't die
for your
sins

—Baldinger

Ballad

In the attic, the poetry
flows into the stagnant
air, the cacophonous vents
threatening to swallow
the art whole and spit
it into the night, which is
where it will end up anyway.

The poets congregate on the
corner of 39th and Bell,
cigarettes and barely-concealed
bottles and talks of revolution
and talks of overdue rent as
the cops and the junkies
and the students and the
homeless make their way
through the mosquito night.

The laundromat tows fast, so
the street is lined with cars
and bodies and vomit and verse,
and the streetlight never quite
makes it past yellow.

An Irish bar lines up the shots,
and a pool cue is the weapon
of choice for those whose lines
are spent for the day.

Some stumble home and some
roll the back roads at minimum
speed, but all will lay their head
praying to the ether that their
fitful sleep will bring the next word.

—Benger

Father's Day

Highwood Cemetery
rush from morning sun
already too hot, I need shade
not looking at my feet
I stumble on the grave of my uncle

I hadn't remembered he was buried here
for a second confused
I look at graves around
Kusserow, a name lost
on the maternal side of my family

I never knew my uncle
he died ten years before
my arrival, kidney failure
barely twenty-one, it's no surprise
that no one really spoke of him
just as now, no one speaks of his other
brother gone, or his other brother gone

I only have some vague story
him placing garlic baloney
on a dog named Seymour's nose
making it sit still
before allowing the dog to flip
the treat, reap the reward

sometimes a day takes you
somewhere you didn't expect to go
as such, it being close, and Father's Day
I figured I should visit my father
who rests in the cemetery next door
whose grave it takes some time to find

in the years after his death
my mother would come here
with her grief, sit on the grass
plant flowers and memories
as my brother and I
played around the stones
counted them, made stories up
while playing Star Wars or G.I Joe

I've not been to this spot often
since my mother remarried
I sit for a while
listen to hawks and jays
the traffic of Marshall Avenue
the blood in my veins
the roots of a tree of history
I came from the rush of this avenue

my sense of time, of place is acute
the way they bleed through memory
become tenuous, because time
and space do not measure
the way we conceive they do

D.A Levy said
I have a city to cover with lines
I consider those lines
I trace those lines
> lines of family
> lines of history
> lines of a city

—*Baldinger*

Just Visiting

I come to you,
sit on your grass,
breathe your air.

There's a tree,
technically a memorial
for someone else,
but I like how it casts
a pleasant shade on
your spot of green.
I lean against the trunk,
you recline as ever.

I wipe the dirt and ants,
curse myself for
not doing it sooner.

Among the barking dogs
and the rumble of a
distant lawnmower,
I read you poetry,
I read you stories,
I tell you of your
grandson,
how sometimes,
I see you in his smile.

I miss you, but the older
I get, the more I
realize you continue on
within my heart and
my head more than you
could ever have known.

A plane passes over,
for a second blotting out
the noon sun.
I picture you above it.

Neither of us bought into
that kind of afterlife stuff,
but it doesn't erase my
whimsical wish.

I rise, dust the back of
my jeans.
You're the one who's gone,
yet it seems that I'm
forever leaving you.

—Benger

Cousins Bar

it could happen on any night in America
a moment when poets take over the bar
the Garth Brooks jukebox dies slowly
to the full barrel of laughter
the explosion of light
that words through the eyes of humans
make. We raise red solo shots
to our memories, to our friends
to the improbability of here
to the humidity of summer
in a borough not in the city
surrounded by the city

we dream out loud
in color tonight
Julio in the doorway
scribbles stardust from pen to journal
Misty and Jenny
dance with their shoulders
to the Talking Heads
Rucci, already famous
rides his five-year-old
rejection from Reading Rainbow
Gegick, Kaldon and the Pajich's
white people dance to Springsteen,

this is working poor joy
it's Friday, we are free
it's everyday and maybe we don't know it
but we are free

when the bar lights cash out
Dr. Wu plays, somehow its moments
on sidewalks lost to time

we cross rivers
we see every day of our lives
they glow ethereal
not because we're drunk
because somehow we're seeing them
the first time, the same with the
quarter wedge moon, the same
with Penn Avenue

oh! the sway
the sway
the sway

Rucci and I talk psychedelics
and words we found under women's tongues
till three am, I give him a gift for his greyhound
we sleep ageless again now
we are light, and we are ageless now again

—Baldinger

At a Hole in the Wall Bar, December, 2002

It was a slow slide.

The night wore on
and the table got bigger.
You hit a point where
you don't care whose tab it is.
Rounds and rounds and rounds.

I fed quarters into the juke box
that had an internet connection.
Pre-YouTube, my eyes glowed at
all the obscure options to which I could
subject everyone in the bar.
Eddie Vedder screamed about raiding a fridge
as the waitress brought a couple more pitchers,
and my dart was just to the right of bullseye,
always only enough off to lose the game.

The idiots at the bar next door
drank Bud Ice from the bottle
and belted out generically bad
karaoke of *Livin' on a Prayer.*

As our table grew,
so did our base;
we soon had a U.N. of drunks,
opinions (but not fists) flying.

Some blue tequila came,
and novice that I was,
I had to be shown the proper
booze-lime-salt etiquette.
I still don't get it.

I forgot to feed more cash into the juke box
so it automatically rolled into Nickleback.
Urged by the table
and my own indignation,
I rushed to wall,
requested some indie-prog from San Francisco.
Chad Kroger gets cut off mid-circle jerk,
and the bartender's pissed.
Who the fuck? she cries,
then cuts the speakers and shouts to the whole bar,
Fuck you all!

The whole table (we've grown to
five tables pushed together,
and I don't know half of their names)
agrees I should complain to the owner.
I decline, refill my glass, order another pitcher,
explain: *Someone gets so upset over something like that,
they've got to have some serious stuff going on.
I'm betting she needs that win,
and I won't take it from her.*

An hour-and-a-half later
we stumbled into rainy two a.m.
Kansas City, off to wherever we needed to go.
I never saw most of them again,
can't even remember half of their faces.

It wasn't till the end of the brief walk
back to my apartment
that I realized I still had
a pint glass in my hand.
I don't even know where that is now.

—Benger

The Night the Fireflies Taught Dave Brubeck to Keep Time

in the bar after a few rounds
she says, *let's take a walk in the cemetery*
better idea, I return
let's go back to my place
roll a joint, THEN go for a walk in the cemetery
her eyes light, she says *perfect!*

it's already past sunset
the pizza shop next door sells beer
wanna split a quart of beer?
how could anyone say no?

she has heard tales of foxes
I have seen foxes
usually at dusk, on still nights
you may hear the pups play
yips and yelps, mingling
bat sirens, nighthawks, whitetail snorts

it's a perfect night to sit in the grass
light rain occasional
we are laughing too hard
telling too many stories
to ever tell if there's foxes

the alcohol, the joint
raise her voice
more manic than its usual
steady huskiness

I want there to be stenographers
for these nights, the madness
of my friends, all these accidental
poets letting their hair down
letting their hearts beat comfortable

we sit, lightning bugs
rise glow steady
¾ time
you swear tonight
is the same night
they taught Dave Brubeck
how to keep time

—Baldinger

This is It

The ash smolders and curls,
twisting into a living thing,
something sentient,
a snake or a worm or something.
It grows, assimilating the cigarette
as the ash inches toward my knuckle.
Then it breaks off and falls to the ground,
a shattered umbilicus, lifeless, done.

We sit in silence in the back of my truck,
me staring at the earthy remains of my smoke,
you looking off into the distance of the street.
Lost in thought, or lost in a lack of thought,
I can't never tell.

You sigh and lay back, stretching yourself
across the rusty old bed.
I turn away from my dead cigarette to
look at you, but you refuse to meet my gaze.

So this is it, I say, or maybe I ask.
I can't never tell.
You don't reply.
I light another smoke.

—Benger

Maybe a Mantra

it doesn't look like August
the green in the cemetery
still unsinged by summer heat
the rains keep coming
it leaves everything lush
it doesn't really get hot here anymore
it doesn't really get cold here anymore

the bank is closed
on Butler street I almost
get t-boned by someone not
paying attention to traffic

the refineries look like heaven
the 62nd Street bridge, Sharp's Hill
lose themselves, time is the equivalent
of nothing, time is nostalgia dying

last night we ushered out a wake
for a favorite bar, we talked about
how many shows and how many dollar
skunked beers we've drank, we are
the age of things that aren't there anymore
we question our moorings, our anchors

I woke up this morning to news
of hate rallies, I'm disconcerted
you will not replace us

you will not replace us?
there is no permanence to this world
we have only a modicum of control
over the lives we lead, I'm sure that's
hard for some people to admit, to exert
force to retain some fleeting control
is madness, an unhealthy sense
that we mean more in the eye of the universe

everything we see here will someday be gone
everything we know will someday be gone
everyone, everything will be gone
I find comfort in that personally

I cross the Allegheny again
follow the S curves up Negley
toward home, I've accomplished
nothing this morning, I have White Antelope's
words in my head, maybe a mantra
Nothing lives long, only the earth and mountains

—*Baldinger*

The Park

Probably the saddest thing
about it all is that
so many of them
never even had
dreams to lose.

Often we think of these people
as having somehow fallen,
taken a wrong turn,
made a bad choice,
lost it all,
and they end up here.

Thing is,
so, so many,
maybe even the majority,
this is their lot.
They've never seen it any other way,
and see nothing wrong with it.

The boy fires off his
neon orange plastic water pistol,
small crack in the seam of the handle
keeps his palm perpetually wet
with lukewarm hose water.

He ducks behind dingy sheets
clipped to a nylon line
stretched between his mother's
and the neighbor's trailers.

The boy's not sure what he's shooting at,
but is sure that the single-wide in the dirt,
all the trailers squatting in the grassless park,
it's all something worth defending.

They boy's mother calls from the door;
something about *shoot them sheets again,
and I'll shoot you, you little shit,*
then recedes to the shuttered
darkness of their shared home.

The boy slinks off into the
stretch of woods that separates
the trailer park from the highway.
He once found a box turtle shell there,
what remained of the animal was
gooey and non-descript,
like alien blood in Saturday afternoon movies.

He hopes to find a baby fox or coyote,
something to call his own,
something that will love him
in the way he loves his home.

—Benger

Jason Baldinger is a poet hailing from Pittsburgh and recently finished a stint as writer in residence at the Osage Arts Community. He's the author of several books, the most recent are *This Useless Beauty* (Alien Buddha Press), *The Ugly Side of the Lake* (Night Ballet Press) written with John Dorsey and the chaplet *Fumbles Revelations* (Grackle and Crow) which are available now. Recent publications include the *Low Ghost Anthology Unconditional Surrender, The Dope Fiend Daily, Outlaw Poetry, Uppagus, Lilliput Review, Rusty Truck, Dirtbag Review, In Between Hangovers, Your One Phone Call, Winedrunk Sidewalk, Anti-Heroin Chic, Nerve Cowboy, Concrete Meat Press, Zombie Logic Press, Ramingo's Porch, Rye Whiskey Review, Red Fez, Mad Swirl, Blue Hour Review* and *Heartland! Poetry of Love, Solidarity and Resistance*. You can hear Jason read poems on recent and forthcoming releases by Theremonster and Sub Pop Recording artist The Gotobeds as well as at jasonbaldinger.bandcamp.com

James Benger is a father, husband and writer. His work has been featured in several publications. He is the author of two fiction ebooks: *Flight 776* (2012) and *Jack of Diamonds* (2013), and two chapbooks of poetry: *As I Watch You Fade* (EMP 2016) and *You've Heard It All Before* (GigaPoem 2017). He is a member of the Riverfront Readings Committee in Kansas City, and is the founder of the *365 Poems In 365 Days* online poetry workshop and is Editor In Chief of the subsequent anthology series. He lives in Kansas City with his wife and son.

www.ingramcontent.com/pod-product-compliance
Lightning Source LLC
Chambersburg PA
CBHW020128130526
44591CB00032B/569